D1374012

Jerald Bullis

ADORNING THE
BUCKHORN
HELMET

ITHACA HOUSE
ITHACA

I acknowledge with gratitude the editors of the following
publications, in which sections of *Field and Stream* first
appeared:
Beloit Poetry Journal: stanzas 22 & 34 (under the titles "Bees
and Spiders" & "Royal Flush")
Poetry Now: stanza 32 (entitled "Buen Viaje")
Tropos-Revue: stanzas 11-17
Western Humanities Review: stanza 35 (entitled "Sentence"),
reprinted in the Borestone Mountain Poetry Awards *Best Poems
of 1975.*
Wind: stanzas 3-5 (entitled "Moving Out")

Adorning the Buckhorn Helmet was written in La Paz, Baja
California Sur, in 1973. I thank the National Endowment for
the Arts for a grant which enabled me to live in La Paz and
write the poem.

Copyright 1976 by Jerald Bullis
ISBN 0-87886-069-x

Publication of this book was assisted by a grant from the
Coordinating Council of Literary Magazines and the New York
State Council on the Arts.

Cover photograph by Tom Neff.

ITHACA HOUSE
108 North Plain Street
Ithaca, New York 14850

Ithaca House Books are distributed by Serendipity Books, 1790
Shattuck Avenue, Berkeley, California 94709. Orders should
be submitted to them.

CONTENTS

What reasonable man ever supposed that ornaments were
something outward and in the skin merely, — that the
tortoise got his spotted shell, or the shellfish its
mother- o' pearl tints, by such a contract as the
inhabitants of Broadway their Trinity Church?

— Thoreau, Walden

ADORNING THE BUCKHORN HELMET

i

Let the meadowlark mount from its own breast like the ox-eye daisy,
Let it lave its hallelujahs from the raptor's eyrie;
Let the watercress fly up and cling to the knotbadged locust
Tree, and commence in the lapse of the wind to wave itself;
Let the buckwheat showy-golden on the stony hills
Sprout its furry leaves in the moist swale with the bluebells,
For nature is not the dull green thing which stands in the way,
Though blinded cripples at desks squeak the squeak of deformity,
Having never flown out through the glass of factuality,
Or felt the rut in the brain that flaps itself loose and says

Nature is imagination itself.
For I have descended walking in the usual woods,
Have trended left down the pitch of a known slope's barren
Fern beginning to rust in the nightchill burring of fall,
And addled as reason, hollow as a locust shell, have felt
And turned right down a way I had never found before, --
I had never found had I bound myself to the paths of the known, --
And following that liana stippled with pearforked promise
Came to the pool of a creek edgemazy with flowering lily,
Where the sweetwhetting of the cedarbirds brindles the light,
And stripping myself of the mannerly and meek,
I knelt to myself in my barrenness rippling the streamstones,
Acting in accord with rhythms I did not know were in me,
And beheld my head abristle with the tines of the mirrored bankoaks:

So it was I came to myself and the play of this adorning;
And in the calmlight dawning between the beams of my dedication,
Blue as the eveningcoronas of ghostviolets over snow, I sang

This is the headgear I must wear, this outrage archaic
As trees, with sabrelengths of tine, and nine tines to a side,
Is what I must adorn and wear with an outworn pride,
No matter what is worn in the land of golfballs,
Or sanctioned by the flowchart of the heart

ii

There was a time when I had nothing: I sat in the midst of my nothing
As a bad hound bellies the ground of his failure, rolling his eyes
Like a man; but there was no one to shoot me:
I had come unto a time of most serious abandonment:
The roll of the eye did not mirror the ragespittle of any master
Or friend It seemed I would have to bring some unholy visitation

Upon myself, as with a man who is not worth shooting
It was as if I were a man
Who heard his children cry with hunger, and laughed; or one
Who sees his wife too heavily burdened, and kicks her out
Of the abundance of his insufficiency; or as if one
Entered a garage, in the first of spring, when the adder's tongue
          blossoms
Bloom hangdog in nests in the shade, and got in the car unaware
Of growth from the ghosts of the wheatcorn, plowed-under cornstalk
And leaf, and engaged the ignition, and watched in the rearview mirror
The exhaust carbon bloom in the sun, iridescent as stagnant water,
While the pistons spoke unspeakable mutilation in the heart
Of the engine, a plaintgreep of winter; and a spider fell
Gut dangling down from the sunvisor, darkly
Suspended, the tuberous body noseclose, livid with young

So there was a time when I had nothing, and hunkered away
From the sun in the rabbity dank, rotten as high game: now I
Go seeking rhythms for the doe's unimpeachableness,
The doe cropping alfalfa, or the one I saw November last
Edged out of woods, her nose thrust into a fieldcorn stalk,
Chomping noisily; a car passed by the other side of the cornfield:
She wouldn't deign a flicker of her shanktucked banner

2

She knew she was invisible in the glove of twilight --
And loudly raggled amid the corn, a hungry woman, --
I can think of no reason for adding this, but tie
It on: give it to the leftside browtine.

iii

Yea let the substantial come forth,
Gallivant at the field's edge and boldly feed: I would like
To see it there, ever and ever, boldly feeding,
Grandiloquent of presence, capable of quick flight --

Let the deer swim in the mist of the dawnbroken wood,
Let the partridge bulk alertly, craning its neck from the tama-
rack, ready for blustering escape at any second;
For I'm pleased with the partridge, the acrobat of the poplars,
The one who keeps a tree between himself and danger,
For his sophistries of exit dispense lessons unbeknownst to him,
And I sign my presence by his booming out of the pines;

Let the ermine slink like a giant mouse in its pelage of March;
Let the porcupine gnaw highup in the hollowdark spruce, speckling
The ground roundabout with curious scats --
A black spiny presence if ever there was one --
But nothing to flap-up fright: a thing
Merely garbed in its necessitous habiliments, like all of us;
Let the rattlesnake wake in the wayoff deep of my boyhood,
Sluggish with winter, its back grayrubbed like gumbark,
A contrary freckling finitely wound down under the shumake,
A fanged and glittering one encircling tendrils of shumake;
And let these various mysteries plume the rightside browtine.

iv

For there are times when you know in a dreamblaze light impaling
    the cornea,
When you are struck out of sight and speech by say

3

The whitetail browsing the nightwealth of alfalfa, when you know
Like a victim of conversion, a twelve-year-old girl hefted
Out of the river slimy with the blood of the lamb, with the
    knowledge
Of the blind -- when you know as the owl's gaze fails in the first
Lightburst of dawn, how words don't work;
How there is no way to rest
With the grayfox sleeping in the silence of ferns, no way
To drift toward the rainy hill with the spike buck at moonset,
Or dance with breeze-taken bracken the onset of spring: how the
Lichen and the rose make do is their own going, or the buff
Puffs of quail chicks, how they survive:

Oh these are the stanzas in stonegrain,
Where the cottonmouths whortle like larks, but not to our hearing;
Where at the edge of the clearing, where blueberries shade the moss
And juncos, sparrows, and purple finches fling from the small
Firs, the obscene dead scattered by hawk
Or shrike, with loops of drawn gut shiny in the undergrowth,
May -- but not to our calling --grow
Whole once more, take wing, and play with the chestnutsides
In the green of the slashings, or, in the fallen
Aroma of orchards eat, and sing!

I'm far from the place where speech blossoms with the white
    flower
Of silence, but hang the declamation
Of sideleapt error here, where
Clearings from time to time blaze suddenly hazeless as whole sight;
For nothing is won to unity
Except where the human heart wracks-to-flowing from the binds
    of its comb
The honey annulling the sting of mutability:
So may these verses adorn the leftside second tine.

For I'd plume the gaudy springresurged autumnaugmented
Boneblood of the whitetailed buck;
The gnarls of length snarlsprouting like tag-alder sprouts
Along the songclosed circle of the mainbeams;
For the antlers gather the heft and bristle of their magnificence
As the wild miracle under them prevails
Through the winters of his enduring; prevails out of the rigor
Of his separateness -- nervous at the freshness and candor of buzzards
And the scruffy ratchet of the jay, discrete
Beside the amative jumble and enterprise of maggotry,
The chronic spooling of rattlesnakes
In the umber and yellow speckle-dark flagrant with summer --
Beyond the commonalty of the garden-plaiting quail,
The yard-daubing banties, lame raccoons haunting libraries,
The accumulation of bleakness around the wellused trail:
Prevails where the woodspider twinkles its way through a hillside
Bed of skullcap, where the kingfisher's still as a blue
        spruce stob, --
I'll attach this to the rightbeam second tine.

Once, when I was baling hay in Missouri, under
The bloody socket of summer sunset,
When the moon is up and low above the ragged snagging of timber,
White as the haunch of a springtime swimmer cottonmouth struck
And drowned, we say a bludgeon-fat copperhead bunch
And slather away from the baler, off to the left in the row
We'd next come down, just boys on the wagon
All joking too-loudly together, and what catches
Inside caught like breaking stitches, for none of us
Wanted the bale that rotten onion, textured like a live --
boiled cat, would be in, a phlegmy darting in the heart as the
        tractor
Swung around -- or we hoped that whatsoever we would
Never desire, if we should receive it, would be baler-ripped
Abundantly through Jesus Christ Our Savior, that

Being justified by his grace, we should get home;
For we all knew of the man become as wheatseed in the ground,
A dreamswole enrichment of the nights of our tommorrows, who

Hefting the bale of the just and the unjust
Stirred from the worried bindings of its dark a too-lithe sorrow,
And came thereby to peace with something
Entering like a judgment through the eye.

I don't know what to make of such a memory,
But look at it here, for here's where I tie it down:
Tight to the leftbeam third tine.

vii

It is night: music drifts to me from the malecon,
The song in Spanish, a male voice, the voice and rhythm strong.

Now the song has changed, same singer, rhythm quiet-sloshy
As ebbtide, but rising up into the ploration of a wail,
Like the radiance of spirit tufting an egret's back.

I don't go to the door, or out to the windy palmtrees
Barked just under the flaring of their fronds like pineapples,
But I begin to wander. Let song be made of candor,
For it's candor clear and strong I hear in the voice of the singer;
And what does the put-up job bring home to anyone?
If we are to rise silvery with anything of clarity,
If we are to wander near the glad auras of our hopefulness,
If the grass is to be green even in our imagining,
Then we must spell out plainly how the pelican stands
Alert and full by the dumped roils of fishgut, how the man
At the corner accepts the tequila bottle from his friend,
Takes a pull, then blooms his cheeks and turns to the wall to
        puke;
How the flighted egrets pellucid against the startle of dawn
Fan-out into the grottos of our bat-hanging day;

6

If we are to lend one grace note to the galaxy of the waterbead
We must tell beyond all carping
How the gospelling trove in the air wears wings of doubt and fear,
How the deer cluster in the frozen swamps of our surfeit
Or drift down into the hollows velvet-antlered with dawn;
How sometimes the sentence fails, the head falling luminous
With the magnitude of loss: if we
Are to get anywhere, if we are to bear the luck-given
Mountains of light, then the spirit
Must groom itself in the Abaddon of the horse-laugh,
Crawl carefully toward the slat that gives on the spaciousness
Of dark, clasping nothing in secret as it goes;

For there can be no secrecy in the practice of art,
And the adornment I make here is my manner of walking naked.
Let this adorn the right side third tine.

viii

It is a long drive out of town, going south, into good country,
The highway sinuous, difficult to drive it seems to the child riding
As nightcrawlers are to snake onto the curve of a fishhook,

An anguish of wiggling, a bit of brown wet burping out
Of where the hook bites, the worm's tail thrashing, the segments
Shuffling under the touch, like something athrash in the brain,
No sign of self but thrashing, the curves sinking deeper into
    woodland,
The blue-green swash of roadside timber deep in groundcreeper,

Then a turn off to the left, a stretch of back
Country road following the cottonmouth route of Marble Creek,
A hayrick sweating in the frostless dawn by a field lane, and a
    crow
On a fence post hunkers as the car approaches,

Sets wing, and flights against a scythe-windrow of wind,
Heading south with the car for a moment, then slipping

7

Onto the blade of the current, cawing behind us, going off:

It is easy to get lost here: from Taum Sauk Lookout
Or Crane Pond Lookout looking south there is nothing
Much for fifteen-twenty mile
But black-green Ozark undulance;   and if you get into it
Walking, there are mossed-over granitic out-croppings, rock
Flakey with pale scale, tuftings of geologic war
In every bare spot, rough country all the way to Lesterville,
With fingernail-sized wild blue flowers clustering everywhere;

And once, stepping out of the ravelment of timber into a glade,
With a rivulet sprinkling over a cliff to the hollow beneath,
Turkeys burst up all around me, wingwallops like shotgun blasts,
Iridescence of wingback and neck tingling with sunlight,
And one great tom -- an easy thirty-pound gobbler --
His double-beard swung black in the air like a scalplock,
Fell away from the flock in a long slow drift to the valley
Of woods below me, merging at last with shadow a mile
Away: I see him now, I would merge with my boyhood again,
I pray for the serious playfulness of the childhood eye,
The light the grown-up path blackens with ignorance early,
The path falling too-quickly straight from the gray heights,
Where snaklings play about their mother in the gray sunlight.
Let this adorn the leftside fourth tine.

ix

I return to my former walks repeatedly --
Going mid night to where the sun breaks down through
        cottonwood
Leafage -- return as now, to water, the stream crisping blond;
Where, under rocks and the cliffling of the facing bank
Roughed tropically with fern, the runnel's chicory-mottled,
And minnows flicker the goldtinged walnut and black: here
        birdsong
Is a variable constant: small yellow
Birds, just a smidgen's worth bigger than hummingbirds,

Flutter chirrups and squeaks through the greentaggles of
    bankgrowth,
And the desert quail, their calls pure as the line of yuccaspires,
Unseen along the talus, in this cliff enchaliced moment,

Call and call.
                    This is a region that does exist,
But I'm not the one to explain what is beyond explaining --
The risen moon is twice as large riding near the earth,
Fat with a propinquity to our wobbly way,
Than when it's flown beyond the touch of birch and fir:

So I study the assertive waves, the ternskimming fluctuant
    ridges,
The incoming tide speaking against the ledges of the headland,
Breaking the profligate vowels of its surge
Over the oystercrusted stacks;
So I study the wind's assertions in the sundown willows,
And the dendritic runs and gouges of the mountain streams
Singing away from their branches toward the sea's mother-root:

These speak a region that does exist,
That is careful of a tendance beyond more local cares,
That seeds and falls, cuts and mends, sheds and fills
On and on, available to our coming and going always,
Always here to our visitation, here when we stay away.
Let this adorn the rightside fourth tine.

                           x

For as when in the first of spring, in May three years ago
Four students -- two girls and two young men -- were shot to
    death
By National Guardsmen at Kent State University in Ohio,
Which he knew then to be more filthcharted than the Thames

(Woe to the puss-mouthed anti-spirits that've slimewashed this
    crime

And maybe one or two others, for
It's impossible to license crime by parts, to favor
Injustice at all, and hope to regulate the measure
Of it: hence presidents are chiefs of criminals,
Askew-eyed toadys of idiocy
Who make the acreage of a city's sewerage seem
Cologne; whose earthly mansions are gargoyled with the limbs
Of children and old women -- whose mothers wombpuked them
        forth
To draggle the snailslick of their maggotlust
-- But to put it so is a slander to the snail and maggot --
Over the generations that have failed
To resent a million million affronts to themselves, as if
It were the signature of nobility to forbear)

And, like a drunken spittlegob on the guilt-trashed sidewalk,
Like the wormed convulstion used for a brain --
A corporate ganglion -- by panderers
Of Interest and Policy and the lye of Honorable Peace,
The spirit shrivels to less than itself, a mote swirling
In blood, forgetful of the mountain laurel and checkerberry --
Still profusions that keep their green in despite of winter --

So any affecting human event may infect our eyes
Against the eternal: let this adorn the leftside fifth tine,
Where the grebe will be diving when These States shall be no
        more,
And the turnstones thriving in the ruddy waters of moonrise.

                    xi

I behold Whitman in the tag-alder of autumn where I walk;
He comes to me in a yellow beard of blooming mullein,
Walking the way his lines sprawl out too long for a page,
Extending his hand as broad as the mullein leaves in spring:
He doesn't speak to me of the wrongs he suffered from grubbers,
How he lost jobs for writing frankly of human love:
He doesn't speak to me of family sufferings, --

                    10

The usual cant-hooks of foundering affection, madness,
Needy brutality, love and refractions of love
Though the murk we flourish or perish in, all of us,
The flowage we rondure with wonder or sink to the compost of;--
But he asks how I get on with the Atlantic coast,
And so I do a curvett or two on my osprey's wings;
Then I take out of one backpocket the heavy-beamed moose in
     Maine
I've saved for such an occasion, its
Antlers spreading from alder to alder spanning the road,
And I tell him the story I've nurtured for accompaniment;
So he laughs and asks how I get on with the Pacific,
And a lean gray poise of heron comes flappingly out of my other
Backpocket: I show it hunting the shallows,
Such delicate expertise, so gaunt with specialization,
Its neck and beakhaft head jodding this way and that,
The Tennessee toothpick of beak spearing sanguine with light;
I reach out a bucket of butter clams from the Sea of Cortez,
Two small octopi found in fantail shells, a handful
Of limesized Mexican lemons: we shuck
And cook-up the batch and don't talk much while we eat . . .

He notices what I have half-adorned,
He doesn't seem surprised; I fancy commendation
In his frank appraisal; he pulls a sprig of mullein out
Of his beard for a chew; the cookfire dies toward the fluency
Of night:
               Some, the clever-smitten, may cock the thing on
          their necks
And speak of rust and mildew, what's in this week or out,
As if the tantivy of maple-livery in fall
Wore lavender galluses one year and sombreros the next,
As if they had looked through nature, or carefully at it –
Splaymouthed harpers of fashion
                              (fire-shadow bristles his speech)
Who can't distinguish underwear from Imagination.
These frame the laws and man the canons that destroy
Possibility, as if they could foresee the modes that spirit
Takes in men; as if they could foresee what ghosts will rise

Up to new life, wherever a self proceeds in its own rhythm!

. . . Now I find my self alone in an oaktree shaking with joy.

Unlooked-for comes this adornment for the rightbeam fifth tine.

xii

The deer came out of the woods, near me, in the dusk:
Crunching the snow on the outskirts of vision, ensepulchered
By twilight, ghosts astir, gliding
Out of the coverts, the marshbeds, toward the midwinter
      cornfield, --
The stubble of cut-over shocks, moonmisted, gray
In the vitreous bloom of a full moon: browsing slowly it seemed
Toward open ground, the snowy pro-
vender -- like something seeking speech, not-quite-remembered . . .

Life is a covert of blessings, as when one is graced with the sight
Of the fat brown woodspath spider;
But where the commonalty waddles, such marvels are rare.
The buck that walks in the dream of the hunter avoids the
      roadside.

So many a one who has turned his way from the broad road
Has done so not for hate of salt, but hate of the baitlick,
Has done so not for hate of honey (or what rhymes with it)
But hate of rabble: we have all seen rabble: the patently
      frippered
Gigolos of fashion's fart-high vision, --
Those with ideas, if you or I could cut through the tinselled
Pus to see them, that would stink a maggot off a gutwagon;
Those who would kiss the ass of a turd
If it were fly-blown with attention, and offered a smell;
Those with spirits a thousand times more foul than a cancer --
Though as busy -- a cancer fed by the cessglut of their hearts;
Those who repay good work with a calculated favor;

12

Who smile by day, but rave at night in the muskegs of their
    dreams;
Who argue with the unarguable
Because their marrow's cancerous with devices of envy --

Rather take to the separate places, the dark declivities,
The ridgepoints brangled with briar-growth,
Where the leaved pools gather vintage from the whippoorwill's
    nightcry;
For the great buck's seignory-branchings are a product of diet,
And of survival: let this adorn the leftside sixth tine;
For the deer is not a portrait of civility,
For the language of his gait has the rhythm of instinct,
Is instinct with a rhythm lovelier than the civil,
And expresses a dark knowingness of the cougar and the wolf;
For the deer is no moralizer,
The deer is not froward to improve your character, though
Saint Hubert flung a cross between the springstag's antlers;
But a vision of does grazing among appletrees in the shade
Of a firegutted farmhouse does no harm;
Nor is the deer an instructor of manners --
Who follows him will grow used to the dew-sparkled scatclot,
As well as drier embodiments of aloofness, for this
Is the manner of leave-taking for the shy;
You owe the deer no duty he will recognize,
And tame ones become scabrous and unfit to behold,
And coddling is a killer of the herd,
It proliferates weak lineage;
The rack-flourishing buck is nourished
By obscurity, afraid of open ground, and not averse to snow.

xiii

These gray creatures -- gray, gray -- the morning growing gray
(I am back now in a particular morning I recall,
The storm a little while passed, the woods still-steeped in wet):
I think of the deer I have seen, I anticipate their coming,
The doe licking its halfgrown fawn in belly-high shumake,

The buck thrashing around and grunting
Down in the marsh-swale, the doe having none of it though,
Running feareyed under the tree where I've taken my perch to watch
     them:
The buck flaunting up a minute later,
His neck swollen with rut, the musculature of his shoulders
Rippling in tune to the musk she left in her scutting wake;
The gray carcasses hung by the antlers in the yards of farmhouses;
The severed heads on a meatpole, topped with a new fall of snow;--

And a ruby-crowned kinglet wingchitters in, tilts on a twig,
Seeming not to mind me, whirping an advance notice
Of day; grackles rise and fall out over the marsh,
Blooming and settling in tandem flocks (and not so tandem),
Heckling away the dark; crows haw far-off, jawing
To each other in their dawnalert way,
Heading out in squads for the sleepy pickings of farms;

Now in the grayrimed firths of light the woodpeckers start
Their clips of chop for the drowse of grubs,
And the kleiny burghers of the brush tangles, foxy sparrows
And chats, and mousequick fluffs of wren,
Begin to rustle the undergrowth, furtive as daycaught goblins,
Flipping their chestnut pennies into the alder-brakes; . . .

Now the sun halforbed in the gapnest of the hills
Joins its con-jer-reee to the morning's becoming --
As if it were just a chick and not the king of the racket,
A new bird shaking dry from the time of its mother-wet --
Its crescent-red edgeruffed with buff
Like the epauleted wing of the redwing blackbird, --

And the squirrels bray Niebelungenlieds from the oaktops,
And the sandhill cranes rise up in the flare of their cries
Over the tussocky reaches of the fresh-water rushes

And the maple wakes on its mid-marsh rise in its roosterhackles,
And there is too much, too much for any hunter, -- and the deer

Have bedded elsewhere, the sun falling
Smoky on their fur!
                    --Let this adorn the rightside sixth tine.

Come out of the narrow ways where praise is clipped by sameness,
The brambleless confinements, hateful angularities,
Where excess is crippled by rote and grass hedged-in with concrete,
And nowhere burgeons the flower of the Devil-May-Care.

xiv

But I'll predict a thing or two before I go:
When the heads of the poor are no longer favored by law for
        cracking,
When negroes may sit as if their dolorous crime for being
Black men and women, fucked-in and fucked-out as the rest,
        were forgot;
When all who are wealthy pay taxes,
When students will give more thought to a thought than to a
        weed;
When writers will say **what** they feel, and damn the magazines,
And return to their duty of praising from the mountain-tops
(One to a mountain -- no coteries or other factions);
When congressmen wear the gentility of well-heeled crooks,
And senators stump for thrush-votes in Missouri's woods,
And a man may walk a city without a fear in his pocket,
And used-car salesmen no longer tell dull jokes in bars;
When cocktail parties turn honest as quick-eyed whores,
(And her pimp not peel your wallet while you're giving her
        what-for)
And wives take this year's style to the bin for charity,
And the cliff-notch in malice not bring the usual tumble, --
When the rancher sets out a ripe sirloin on his fence for the
        eagle,
And the eagle struts up like a lawyer and takes a bite;
When weasels neglect the habiliments of presidents,
And varmit poison's allowed in the watering-holes around
The capitol; when television
Finds substance beyond its bowel-movements,

15

Deodorants, palliatives for excess, and drugs against the fear
It lulls the populace out of year after year after year;
When the person sitting in darkness grows immune to our
    blessing,
And clocks lose their ubiquity,
And the oscillation of waves is the study of stock-brokers: --

When marvels such as these have come to pass, I'll situate
My shotgun up my ass: The Marianas Trench
Will cut a fart; and everyone'll know what's art
And not: let this adorn the leftbeam seventh tine, for
Everything that's well is doing fine.

xv

I say this out to you plainly, as if it were not a poem,
As if I were saying it all late at night to myself, and would
Rather be elsewhere. For what will become of the timebound
    cabins
Of intellections? What will become
Of their wellargued limitations? I have gone out to the mountains
Have climbed the windcreaky towers of rational computation,
And have seen how high our cities affront the atmosphere.

The earth yaws and swaggers its manifold ways at once,
An apportioned sandgrain of a continent
Tidalswagging in a single ridge of tide toward Vega;
And what is Vega? Something we posit as there because
We're flying away. Did you know this mite's precession wobbling
Causes its axis to draw a cone-shaped figure once
In, more or less, 25,800 years?
And what will become of the timebound cabins of intellections?

They stand desolate in the spacious final clearing, weather
Curling the siding free of its construction, useless
To hunters if the buckbrush, shumake, and wild lone apple-trees
Do not surround them, if the ridges go unrhythmed by
The wind asaunter in the gnarl-lyres of oak,

16

If the dawn scatters unwarranted
By the clear allegro of the jays,
If the kingtines of the hickory fail to wimple with dawnshine,
Or the mist not rise like an added silence from the shaken
    silver
Of willows: oh if spirits be organized men
Then they are the world, and the songs they build
Their eternal hutches with define the universe.
For we thrive by the accumulation of darkness round
Our light: by the useable solidity of my desk --
While I stay here with the kingfisher flirting its stub of tail,
Watching for shiners and hogsucker minnows in the dusky veins
Of light -- I attach this to the right side seventh tine.

xvi

But let me not fluster credulity
With what the doubtful would smug-off lightly as rhetoric:
The peregrine already fattens on the pigeons of Manhattan;
Nests in the coigns of short-sightedness,
Casting over the city like an unobtrusive portent:

When Cortez crested the mountain-screen of the Cordillieras,
And descended the flourishing reaches of maize and maguey,
Noting the chinks in the hub-bub of security and repose
Where the lower classes were offered daily in sacrifice,
And the despot slunk in council with his principal parasites,
And sent out useless ambassadors,
While the middleclass ate and drank, looked blank, and ate and
    drank --

Then the gardens of Iztapalapan
Were trellised with creepers and shrubs that numbed the air with
    perfume,
And the paths were shadowed by fruit trees brought from rifled
    places,
Planted by sweat that politic incense dissipated;
There aquaducts channelled the purl of comfort throughout the
    grounds,

And an aviary filled with quetzals and parakeets
Lulled the toadys that lolled a reservoir of stone
Noosed by a walk almost a mile in circumference,
And a flight of onyx steps fell to the water below,
The dispassionate waiting water, which fed
The canals or gathered to flowering in fountains, flowering,
Which diffused what must have felt like a perpetual ease;

But scarcely a generation's eye had winked
And the town itself was deserted, the lake shore strewn with
      house stone,
The encircling plains converted to a flourish of morass,
And the heron concocted its nest on the stob of a palace.

Many are given to history, so I give them this,
For the world is simpler than ignorance gives it credit for,
And cities flute in their garish and fall while the country
      remains,
And men pass on; but the beams of vision abide: abide.
And I plume this from the leftbeam eighth tine.

                    xvii

As when I go to a swamp or desert or river or mountain
To strut with the grouse ruddy-freckled in slats of woodslight
And hunker belly-to-oakmast at my crunch on the ridge,

Or study, askant the black tailtip of the ermine, how it
Gorges at the throat of the hawk by the winter-starved deer,
The featherchaps of the hostbird showing apricot against snow,

Or wraith with dewrise the vagaries of blowdown, up
Through snaggles of twig and leaf, locust-leavings, frogbones
Miraclewashed beyond all self-assertion;

Or rise up out of my husk for a while in the cedar-copse,
Joyous-equable, afloat unthinkingly to the nuthatch's chippings,
Or wander in goal-less random the gametrail's musky with dawn --

                     18

As when I go down to a driftwood perch on the shore and
      delight
In the fiddler-crabs sidling up out of the piddling holes
In my stillness, the smallest ones flicking-out first into the light,

And tell by the way they ball-up their work they know nothing of
      where I should go
                                    (oh though I know nothing I'll keep
An ear tuned for the boundless, that the days of my going may
      touch
On the uncapturable, in the bobwhite's wingwild surety
Or the rutting dragonfly's cry; and when
The drought-twisted antlers of the juniper
Frame the yuccaburst of sunset against eternity's granite
I'll go out to take my pleasure of the moony shucks of the
      sharks,
The thin thin cusps of mouths smiling
At their high smells returned from sunny wandering) --

As when I drift out from my bed in the mid wash of the night
And wander stepping like darkness on the ricegrass and
      rabbitbrush,
Slipping into the vacant sidewinder grottos

For a breather, polishing-up my burrowing owl chitter
For the tarantulas, who skitter their hairy nightmares away
From me, talking it over later under the pricklypear; --

As when I take on moonshine and lay
For a long time on the dorsal leaves of the ridge-oaks,
Listening to the lyrations of the run-off treble
Over the stones of the whippoorwills' lapse and the owl's
      tremolo
Down to the towns and cities the thriving and dying keep

--So l bear in my own person the bosom of heaven and earth:
Let this spurt up -- gaudy, unrefined -- from the rightbeam
      eighth tine.

For I've watched the hunting heron hallowing dawn to the
        shallows,
The petrels rafting up from the stormy inrush of dusk,
Scattering out like decimals toward the mid-sea ledges,
And know no way but this to tally the rhythms of such worth.

                        xviii

The detected murderer carefully injects himself with anthrax,
The blackmailer closes the office-door behind himself
And the doctor looks up, and turns to rust on a scalpel.

The secretary's eyes get swampy after two martinis --
She has a lot of living to do, she hikes-up the skirt
Of her past. The professor buckles into his review, --
He's on to this guy, has detected a wayward plagiarism,
(Four publications more and maybe a shot at Yale)
But the proper quibble doesn't come:
He hears the ghostly economist in the corridor,
A student shuffles in the papers outside his cubicle-door --
He inserts a pink sheet and writes a necessary memo.

The businessman rows toughly away from his ill-named yacht,
The wife puckers in the dinghy-bow in a platinum fit,
The taxi drivers on shore stow their pints and laughter,
The old Indian gets her child in a hungry pose.

Graduate students congregate in their auras of coffee:
One argues with erudite madness that Cordelia isn't
Dead: others calmly peck at the obvious faults.

Two youths get drunk and go to the zoo to taunt a lion,

Ad-men push away from their desks
And gaze out rapt with the nubile reaches of concrete.

The intern extracts the woman's works
By vaginal hysterectomy -- the mess suddenly blooms

Into a private jet lurching toward Cabo San Lucas.

A man rambles unruffled in his plans for the future:
The peninsula's being turned into a gringo-gulch:
He's going to buy a piece of land on the untouched coast
And start a language-cum-survival school for boys.

The bureaucrat luxuriates in the slime of his squalor:
Others will see the wisdom of his failure someday.

The parents wait for the brass of a patriotic return:
How can they know their son, who
Was named by his schoolmates 'Keg-Ass,'
Fell into his reputation a year ago in a rice-field?

The critic endures the public enfilade of his wife:
That night he outlines an essay on **Troilus and Cressida**.

These are a random sampling of the Real World, where the
        Action
Is, where cliches go in and out of the same doors endlessly,
Fondling each other spiritlessly,
Too bored to read sex manuals -- adepts of the naivete
Taught at finishing schools toddle about in the slap
Of common light, looking for some new cause to buttress
Their numbness with -- but I am worse
Than abashed; for whoever walks without sympathy
Walks to his own funeral dressed in a shroud: let this
Adorn the leftbeam's ninth-sprout tine.

                        xix

I am far from Nothingness, the ghost of the pistil unpetalled,
The roots in the marl-less marl of continuum's perfect silence;
(Still howls are safely beyond all condemnation and praise)

I haven't shaken loose at all from the attraction of others;
I'm going to slog right through the brush I already know,

21

Not because I'm tired of the bluejay in the backyard spruce,
Or the spider adrowse in the spiral of one of my notebooks,
Waiting for me to turn off so he can stretch his legs --
I could learn a bit of patience there --
And the jay shot-through with revery
Might say how he braids squalls through bluewhite shrubbery --

But because I want to branch out,
Augment the imperfect sprawltines of this sacrament,
Till the mind sickens with the range inflecting past assessments, --

The milkvetch and hornbeam, popple and buckbriar holding their
        own,
The shrike mewing clear and wirey, its lizard pinned to a thorn,
Everything just the same as before, but different, --

Then wakens out of itself, refurbished,
Returned -- to starmusters peripheryriding peachstone.

For whatever knits in the corner has ceased going on and on.

For I've seen the swagbranched oak, mistbroomed at the edge
        of the marsh,
And think how it once was a pustule popped from the side of
        an acorn,
Lower than ivy and fernwisp, less august than a fungus,
And how its trunk-circumference now has made good the past,
How its roots have tropically fattened themselves with material,
And xylem and phloem fed its sunward limitations,

How part rootrein-imprisoned and part limbwinged, chained
With power and prostrate to an estimable height,
It has flaunted up from the mutable as if it could fly,
A fixed expositor whereby to measure departure,
A true creation gnarled-forth out of next-to-nothing.
If I walked there now I could stop for a kindly
Piss: so I take on the stricture and vaunt of my natural place.

For there's more than enough here to keep me shy of silence,
And time rots every cause whatsoever: oh
Only extravagance is memorable; but we wake
To the daylight of our self-conceit,
As if the stars were less defunctive than at night.

Oh some may think this a crazy and halfcracked
Headgear to adorn and wear through all one's days: maybe it is.
I affix these lines to the rightbeam ninth and final tine.

xx

Here the rockcress blooms, the slender pods hanging downward,
As if what I have I have, as if what is done is done.
And what do I have to give? The best I have is before you.
And if you could see this shaking unsightly about my head
In the way it has come to me here, titmice
Drubbing for grubs on a deadfall-fir between my ears,
A cottonmouth sunning along the curve of one of the beams,
A crane flying with its long legs ruddering level-out behind,
An osprey nest on a bonegall ledge of one of the antlers,
A mooncircle of jackrabbits keening one of their dead --

If you could see my offering thus when I approach you,
How would you greet me then? Would the chipmunk tucking
A nut in the humus bulbous with mushrooms aft of my forehead
Take you aback? Would you offer me a drink? Would
The warrant out for me as a serious person be
Revoked? Would the bullsnake hissing
Out of the October oak's sienna-flocculence ruin
The party?
                    I have been where the geese hwraank hwraank
In a dreamtrove near-above, unseen,
A music from a structureless source, drift-patterned in the night
Air as in sleep, giftstippling the dark --

Where the great horned owl still-hunts the snowcowled thickets,
Perched like a feather-bulb of stob on the lightningslewed pine,
Journeyman-like in his looking, darkening round his hunger, --

23

Or walking the road up to the abandoned farmhouse,
Where the bobwhites flushed by a fox have scattered-out in
    the fencerow,
And bust up singly again as I pass along, giving
It steam for a shotgun's birdshot span,
Then holding their wings to a glide into a briartangle, --

Or sheltered under a mesquite in the nightpatter of rain,
Watching the driftwood cactus-fire,
And a scorpion wasps quickly out of a rockwarmed limb,
The sidelong question-mark of its tail precise in shape,
And I squash it: (so facts are curled beyond us all around us,
Palegreen with hiding, dangerous, till warmed to action)

Along the merciless slap of the coast,
Where just-offshore the blue-crabs wait in their kelplurk caverns,
Or swing with a pinchered left-hook when I tease them in
    tidepools,

Where the osprey ruffles itself at the voltage of my approach,
And hikes-up his gothic backside from the spire of the high
    cardon
And gives a calcareous spurt, before lighting-out --

Listening to the tide steady-breaking up the sleepshoals,
Acts and omissions sloshing something unknown ashore,

The cornstalks flauting in long rows out of the day's lapsed light,
The winter spartling brittle off the poplar-stand,
A convolution shifting slightly in the swimming-hole ledge,
Boyshouts, the leeches clustered under the rockshelf, clarity,

An eagle luffs from a piling, and sweeps
In a low long sweep out over the Mississippi,

The beagle tostles the rabbit, a leg jerks, then it screams,
Somebody crushes its head with a shotgun butt, I loom out

Stepping on moonlight silvering Fletcher's field, hi-there,
A hand I know reaches up out of a cow-patty, --

The body brightens by gasoline-light on the hood of the car,
The feet caught in the windshield. The fire
The fire -- It 'on't hurt him none, he's dead awready --

It is this we come back from to sit in the structured sadness
Of living rooms, to sit with ourselves
And our resembling others, complaining about the weather
As if it had never rained, solicitous of each other's
Shareable secrets; or dogearing the corner of mystery
And pulling-up to a steak, speaking quietly of tomorrow
And the usual propaganda, far-off
Now, from coresilence, but reaffirmed to the breakage
Of the day-to-day: composed about the composure we have
Brought back with us, wearing the buckhorn helmet that
The many will never notice, and,

Strangely glad of this, refreshed.

FIELD AND STREAM

I don't have a vocation to speak of;
I don't have an acorn's worth of juice,
No money in the bank to use

With telling harm against anyone I
Conceive of as my enemy -- I can't put anyone
Away, not even the hag that rises up

In the disfigurement of my house
Sparkly as death or costume jewelry,
As if she'd cornered the market on

The hoity-toity, like a burnt-out starlet
Or muse -- I can't put her away - I don't
Have the jack, to reiterate, to get her

Out of my lair into a posh-house for
The useless, and I also lack the gumption
To sign her into the public-paid-for

Nut-pound, besides which I don't have grounds:
I mean if you hang around all the time
In a backwater muck-slough

And a cottonmouth bites you
Which of the principles are the neighbors
Going to say is irresponsible?

You can see how I'm into what I'm into --
I've got to beg this slathering bitch
To bite me every day, then act normal about it --

2

I've got to commingle her fang-pus with
Whatever demands the commingling in me
Then dribble the mess out, in private.

Sometimes I even like it -- hell, I love it:
It's a dis- amounting to a com-
pensation for the lost if ever there was one;

And saying that frees me to beg for things
From her -- get down on the elbows of what
I call my wings and -- to be frank -- wax

Piteous -- that I can't get in a whore house
Or a drug store: -- Give me a lyric poem of
Ceremonious effect -- my eyes fluxed with need-

slick -- I say to her: let it embcdy
A complex thought, or emotion; be organized
By elaborate argument, illustration;

Characterized by impressive length, cantilevered
Diction -- all in all a serious or -- I know it's
Too much to ask for -- exalted tone;

Let me get into an old form and shoot
Off so homostrophically loud and long
(Not an occasional piece)

That she (it) becomes the medium of
A calm, ah, of a completely -- it's
Too hard to wait -- modern content.

3

That's one way of beginning: another
Is to say a poet works out his country.
It is like hunting. He takes game there,

He gets to know it with a calm, rational
Thoroughness; but he will still happen
Upon things there

That he never expected to see: it may
Be a porcupine big and blackbristly
Looking, looking big as a bear

Up in the high gloomcaves of a large
Pine tree; it may be in winter
Far enough north, a snowy owl

That, not seeing you standing there, will
Light on a stump nearby, a miraculous
Scurfy creature, the white plumage

Peppered with black, the breastdown
Yellowish, the color of snow where deer
Have freshly pissed; it may even be

A deer: a buck so big you never dared to
Hope he'd be where you were -- say
A whitetail with nontypical antlers

(That's what I'd like to see), the points
Askew and asymmetrically apportioned, twisty,
Maybe one of the browtines bowed out as far

4

As the nose like a unicorn's horn --
The beam spread a full thirty inches -- give
It eighteen points at least, or hell

Thirty-six: let its head look like
An oak tree, an old one, moving here
And there (in my vicinity) about three

Or four feet off the ground. That's what
I'd like to see -- I don't know what you'd like
To see. I walk around in my mental wilderness

(The only wild place left) trying to scare up
Something noeminal, something we can share,
Something we know in the salt-slosh of all our cells,

That were born so unaccountably from
Broken-down rock and virus. Is it accidental
That Noemon was the name of the fellow

Inspired by Athena to supply
Telemachus with a ship to search for Odysseus?
Fortuitous that "noetic" (Gk noêtikós intelligent)

Is right under the fellow's name in
My dictionary? The house is a mess --
Mother (eorþan moder) can't handle it --

Sharpers are sucking up the lobster bisque
And suckling pig, wreaking havoc among
The cream puff shells and tangerine cream tarts

5

That my father, wherever he is, paid for,
Is paying for. I'm set to set out --
We need somebody here who can string

His own bow, get tough with the wine-bibbers,
Show the hackle fly heroes, the brunch party
Cowboys, how things ought to be done --

Flip an arrow through a row of axe-head
Haft-holes for starters. But what I started
To say earlier was that a poet works

(And hard) out his country: doing that he
Gets to love things that other people find
Merely uninteresting (chipmunks chirruping,

Cleartoned, at the woodsedge side of a berrypatch,
Mists ghosting up from corn for acres and
Acres off toward the horizonwoods, jays

Jaysquawking in a variety of scabrous ways,
Chickadees that just whirr in and almost
Light on your head --! little black beady eye!

Small as birdshot: squeak squeak der-der-der);
But periodically he gets the feeling that
He's worked all his country out -- that nothing trove-

shot-through is going to happen to him in there
Anymore: so he has to open up a whole
New country for his solitariness to move around in.

6

Play me a gauche dulcet, affetuoso,
Just one: Now as I was hung and
Queasy under the nippled boughs . . .

LOVE, in the stunted beachtrees' quailing
In the tidebreeze fealty to the sun,
Near the sea and the concrete bunker

Like a coastlodged bone sloshed
By a hodgepodge of waves and kelpwisp,
Just offshore; with the fox sparrows

Shekling the weathershingled roofs at the head
Of the bay where, by the light of the heaven
Of memory, seven snowy egrets are

Sighted again, for the song of the consecration
Of this day: on a spit's worth of island
Where killdeering plovers spear, amid

Boomerangling gulls and other
Featherlings of the shoals, all
Sprinkled with lightgold again in the loops

And splays I lend for the time of my
Singing against the inevitable
Desiccation, the stone ground

Down to sand of the trodden harbors and wharves --
I sought you, in a plighted grappling, prelude
Of flight and dancing to this daily

7

Taking of miraculous bread and wine: oh
I entered into covenant with you. AND
We engaged by the aid of the Holy Spirit

Abiding in the musk of the lilies of
The valley that now sweeten our mutual
House, and by the violetbursted chivespines

Of our garden, and by the witchery of tracery
In the purple and yellow and white of our hill's
Wild iris; and by the lowly dandelion

31

Which, rooted up before its blossoming, renders
Its blessing tenderly in a mess of cooked greens;
And by the appletrees in flare and the flux

Of cherrybloom misting the gnarling of fruitlimb,
We engaged to walk together in our love:
From where we stand

Let us go on, go on,
And with joined hands;
For we lie not down in all

Our days amid amaranth,
Nor attend the zitherish dither
Of holier lyres

Than we wake out of the provenance
Of devotion, by the reconciliation
Of sundered flesh. -- And Horace was right --

8

To die for your country, to get
Your horns and get a chance to use them,
Is sweet and -- if you get that

Far -- fitting. Decorum: working it
All in feateously -- a compaction energy
Rich, like a black hole in space, where

When everything thereabouts gets hot
Enough, Pow! and we grunt to the heights
Of our heritage, head and heart lost

In the light years of our coming
By way of thermonuclear combustion,
The Big Bang spew after several

Billion years of fore-play recapitulated
On a time-scale and by bodies we
Can grasp, all observers lost, the self

Dying to experience, over and over again,
That loss (and gain) of the world, the self. --
"We penetrate bodily this incredible beauty" --

And Emerson's right: it's a holiday,
A royal revel, the proudest most
Heart-rejoicing festival I've ever decked

And enjoyed. It's not very halcyon today:
Robin flights get warped by the wind
And the rain's forced the worms up

9

To where the robins could -- if it weren't for
The wind, which must make hearing a worm
Hard -- eat them: joyously beak them

Out of the flooding wormroads under the grass,
The worms grappling tight by their heads or tails
To the last piece of earth they'll ever get,

Qua worm. It wasn't very nice yesterday
Either: especially in Arkansas, north Texas
And Oklahoma, where a few tornadoes

(Twenty-three lives' worth -- human) showed
I hope to the best of their ability
How you can get rubbed wrong, on

The short run, by nature's benignity.
Still, the girls are peddling everything they've
Got down and up the street outside

33

The wirey reticulation of my window-screen;
And now that it's getting on toward twilight
The sun's lightening in patches

The still windy extremities of the trees --
Mostly elms. Those people down in Oklahoma,
Etc., found nature to be the circumstance

That dwarfs every other circumstance, just
Yesterday. They got the "gates of the forest" in
A big sway: the knapsack of custom blown clean away.

10

I'm afraid of being guilty of nonfeasance --
I'm more afraid of that than of going too far:
I want to walk naked in the Big Woods

Of my saying, come out lost -- scared
And wondering -- in marsh swatches rhythmic
With relations I can't by logic apprehend,

Can't foreordain: I don't want to be
The Frederick Goddard Tuckerman of the Space Age.
I'd rather by the Walt Whitman of

Crane Pond Mountain (Clark National Forest,
Missouri Ozarks) or the Henry Thoreau
Of Navarino Marsh (Shawano County, Wis.)

Or the Christopher Smart of LA, scratching
Rivers and gorges out of grief, that kind
Of soundness, on the piss-odiferous walls

Of Bedlam, if it comes to that. This here is
No attempt at embracery -- you can't embrace
Me, I won't embrace you -- I can't embrace

34

The embranglementa, organized beyond my
Conning, I walk around in thinking about
And feeling (it), that I try for transformations of

To here . . . All langwidge is elliptical (like, given
Our ignorance, nature): this is elk-weed (or
Fire-lily). Tips are an emolument in addition to wages.

11

But you want to know what I'm up to?
You want some slot you can put your dime into
For a dime's worth of hidden meanings? You

Get miffed when certain people ignore
Such humility. Okay: I buy that. You
Get tired of being told that poems are

Incarnations (in-carnations, visceral
Floralities) of the spirit in form --
You get tired of the prophet's severity

Interwhacked with the mediator's urbanity,
I mean you like it when people shit
Or get off the pot -- you're gut-tired of

Arriving at a characteristic perplexity
Of effect -- devastating, boring -- from
Which the tinge of an anaerobic pedantry

Is not absent -- you're plain done-in by structures
Rather anagogically glyphyletic about nothing
There being able to grow, die, or change --

You get bumfuzzled by infernos of memory
Wherein somebody's Aunt Mary gets
Twaddled by the hired man and thereafter

Feels her husband isn't such great shakes --
You like your tropes to rev up sexy and
Click: 'Is grandma coming?' 'No,

12

She's just breathing hard.' Okay: I buy that:
Unknown conditions of temperature, pressure,
And saltiness eventuated in protoplasm --

We came from what the rocks lost
To the moon-swinging deeps, in part at least --
Poetry is a natural science, except that

It's more comprehensive than any natural
Science; but it is a specialized procedure
Whose subject-matter is nature, the whole

Shebang -- even the parts you think you've risen
Above: I attend, yelling, whimperingly yelling,
To the leavings of the fugitive gods:

It's fields and woods, even your garden,
Your lawn -- that's what I have to give,
That's what I'm into. I got tight

Little organizations of violets, interspersings
Of poison ivy, some fungus starting on
Lightning-jismed birch, areas of swamp

The wind plays the larch nooks and willows of
Even when your care is elsewhere: I got
The soil the spider forages that

The partridge berry broomed from
That the ruffed grouse ate, gloried in
Till the weasel caught him napping --

The weasel the horned owl whomped in the snow
That became the water the earth needs,
That the partridge berry is fighting for:

I got the strewn feathers of the horned
Owl that died a-tangle
In the brambles the fox runs through:

So much still to be discovered, so much
To which adjustments will have to be made, --
I'm wound up; I don't know when

I'll stop; I'm talkin bout mo than
Just the human fambly, brethren, sistren --
We got to take wider views of the universe,

As I think it was Thoreau said. --
The Foul Fiend Flibbertigibbet's in
Your waste can -- there's hardly a heath

Left to get cold on these days --
Don't come telling me how you're going
To borrow $100,000, whip-up a fancy

Restaurant that'll out-chef the fat
Flank of the gaudiest competition, and
Send Marshall Field announcements of

The opening to the best-appointed loneliness
Pursuers this side of Darien,
Connecticut: your friends. I don't want to know. --

14

We've already got upwards of 400 million
Tons of garbage -- per year -- to get rid of
In These city-festered and want-plotted States --

Take a look outside your split-levelled
And otherwise bifurcated rat burrow --
The only thing you've got new

Is a separation from what's been going
On around here (earth) for something
Like 2.5 billion years -- a separation

So apparent that it's just not real --
If your kid sidles up to you and says
Hubert, you're out of it, just clip

Him on the jaw and say, I know it,
Son, I know it: a whole gaggle of
Archaeopteryxes couldn't have shat

On Manhattan or Coeur d'Alene the way we did,
Do. I'm fed up with being armigerous:
Nature's not exclusive but you've got

To be in or out, and right now we're out. --
I don't know about you, but I want to be in:
I want to take my chances in the warp

Of a universal isotropism so wild
It doesn't even need to go woof.
-- Before the bias and fluence of saplings in windy light,

15

Before the first hawk huddled hovering
In a high wind over
A fearthrottled proto-chicken or -mouse,

Before any slightly depressed area was ever
Spurged with lavender cups of pasqueflower
Bloomluminant with received water from

38

Higher ground; before the buttes were
Yellowtufted with marigold too manifold
Of its elegance to look down on

The pinkfruit flowering dock of the riverbars,
Way off before the first grouse chick
Ever scuttled peepweeping before the lunging

Breath of a skunk or fox; before the first
Wolverine dragged a marmot squiggling screeches
Out of the earth, sometime before the first

Jew got tamped down live by a German,
Head and all, or the first Arab got
Shot in the ass with a mauser for

Stealing gasoline, or the first debutante
Found out where comfort is on a country
Club pool table; before anything got so complex

Everybody thought he ought to ameliorate
The contusion by setting himself up -- in
The singular -- as an organizer, there

16

Had to be some badassed gastropod or arachnid
Telling still lowlier nucleations of getting
And spending where to get off -- some fungus

Talking soothingly to his fellow plants . . .
Oh how little we know of nature, how
Little we know. It wasn't until 1930

That two fellows (forget their names)
Discovered that the "moss" on a snapping
Turtle's back isn't moss at all

But tiny fauns of algae -- the basal
Cell a cleftfoot called a holdfast --
That live in green accord with their turtle.

There are four or five different kinds --
They named that first one **basicladia
Chelonum.** In the forty odd years since

Its discovery, that one's never been
Found growing anywhere
But on turtle shells. Oh it can grow on

Rocks or logs: has been transplanted
And watched; but prefers a turtle to
A rock or log: a simple plant.

We've got sandmobile runnels in the moon's
Mari anguis (did the moonboys go there?)
And are just getting on to the errant

17

Commensalism of a turtle's back.
-- Let me not chortle and growl obscurely;
Keep me from the dense and lovely

Fakery of merely verbal dancing;
The flummery of the glum; grant me
The joy to say straight-out the immanence

Of impermanence; I need help;
I'll keep my stand; stay hobbled
From the loco weed of swish sports cars

And quaint farms and summer resorts
By wellkept lakes and on and on;
I don't need much but I need help;

I'll wait. I'll stay. Particularity
Gospelled out in its particular light
Ought to be obscure enough for

Anyone. I say what I see, I
Keep to myself; I don't help anyone
Much but then a lot of people

Get along untroubled by me too.
There's a toadstool in my mind
That's also under a tree; I don't

Know how it got there -- here: I'll
Leave that to the people who think
Words are berries -- here it is: NYC.

18

It's a hirsute psychological question, I'm told,
Whether sense-perception involves thought;
And, if it does involve thought, what

Kind of thought's in it (that it
Might be said it necessarily involves)?
Well: if feeling's snappier thinking than

Logic can manage, and I'm willing to
Assert already that, at the worst,
It's abundantly different, then I'm

All for it. As I said, I say what
I see: so I can see what I say
And maybe see how my mind's doing

When I don't think I'm thinking but
Only penetrating feelingly this incredible
Beauty (or at least penetration, after

41

A fair spell of dallying, 's my design):
While ago I went out and diddled
Some hawkweed, felt the prickly-skinny

Stems, looked at the red blossoms shifting
Toward gold in the blossom-core, the inmost
Sexy parts -- I touched the whorl

Of rimey-furred leaves, radiating next
The ground, of one of them -- I drew
A bucket of water, pumping the clanky pump.

19

You say there is nothing here: the metropolis
Isn't sustained by the wilderness, and
The wilderness from the vantage of the city looks

Dark, dull and damp, damp and dull: yet metal-stark
Like the bore of dark; that "country" is a wet
Place where lots of birds fly around uncooked.

You say there is nothing here: that Thunder
La Boom would never play at the Buckhorn Tavern,
That if she did the thunder in her la would plop,

The sequins on her flopping booms would wilt,
A lot. So you say there is nothing here:
There is nothing here, you say, going nowhere.

What I like is the emptiness, an emptiness
Deft as the most formal grief, precise
As the jod of a heron's beak in the cove-lilies;

An emptiness like the clarity of rain stipples
On a lake's pelage at noon, a prodigality
Saying nothing much louder

Than a duck's quack from the shallows of
The nightreeds or the nighthawk's midflight
Growl, than the gustage of the wind

A-bramble in balsam or a moth bonking your window,
Bumping against it, night-bumping, from the outside --
In this abandon, this acute abandon,

20

The poem hones its antlers like a buck.
For something in us wants the endless
And unutterable differences, not

The damasked glory of the golden forms,
Not trees in their generic Latin husks,
Not a poet plunking a lyre like Orpheus,

Not 'the house is human, the lightning half-
divine,' not any definition, any bind --
Something in us wants the sayer to say

I drank a cup of coffee, the cup porcelain white,
The coffee steaming black, and looked at
The mounted buckhead looking out of the wall,

Out of the varnished knotty pine of the wall;
And thought of stopping by Ernie Yunk's place
Yesterday, of noticing the twelve-point

Heavy-beamed buckrack on the living-room wall;
Of asking him if he got that hereabouts, of
Ernie saying 'Yes, three years ago, in the big

Meadow up the road: he broke across the open
Running like a horse, and when I hit him
Pinwheeled tumbling end-over-end, three times

Or so it seemed, before he piled up.' Something in us
Wants the white speckles on a sun-blooded
Limb of silver birch, here, the trunkwhite welted brown.

21

Ideas resemble woods in that all of them,
From beanfield fringing lots to oceanic
Opacities of brain-provisioning green, hide

More than they reveal. Leaves, then,
The halberd-shaped leaves of yellow violet
For instance (and, in spring and summer

And for maybe a jot or tiddle into fall
Flowers too -- the yellow blooms in axils
Leafy-bract of the aforesaid violets --

To maintain the violet) or
The dissimilar spear-head leafage of birch,
The leaf edges on this one a little toothed;

Not to mention the styles of pinnation found
In different kinds of oak, in all of which
The venation is feather-like, the veins

Abranch like hill branches from the quills: leaves,
Then, stand -- by trembling, shuddering and
Otherwise flailing in almost solid ranks

Of sameness (per tree) -- at least in their veiling
Capacity, for tradition. The trunks I guess
Would have to be the radical Yea-

And Nay-Sayers that ruck up out
Of the moilure, sucking in nutrients from
A few yards around as they go: I guess so.

44

22

I've been around -- especially around here
For some time now -- and so feel qualified
To say that your common bumblebee,

Too common around here this morning
Anyway, is certainly not a solipsist:
One minute they're playing rings to

My head's saturn, and the next cutting
Didoes over in the cattails and pickerelweed --
Then they'll swing back

By in squadrons of parabolic bee-line
As if I were more like a target than
A race-marker, and flirt up on the hill

Under the big white pines to mess around
With the pine spiderwort and bunchberry.
Unlike the spiders, that are known

To work themselves into cramped toolshed
Corners and to web-up quixotically in
The plop-zone of outhouse holes, the bees

Get out and bother things, not a little like
People hell-bent to broaden themselves;
Just yesterday they were taking

A ground-sessioning orgy of flamboyant-
hackled butterflies for flowers: it was a riot.
I've never seen a spider do that.

23

"To think truly is to think freely."
(Nature and Man, Paul Weiss: NY, 1947)
Is that reversible? To think freely

Is to think truly. I think so; I also
Believe, as I've intimated already,
That you can just haul off and come

Close to something better than Aristotle
Or The Truth if you embrace
Much (a lot) of what Our Heritage

Asks us to keep at a distance.
I've been looking at the **Oxford**
Anthology of English Literature (for instance)

And one thing I've noticed there
Distanced to an attentuation that escapes print
Is something about how flora and fauna,

Ragweed and snakes, fuck -- you'd think maybe
Diatoms, those tiny aquatic plant cells
That come by the millions (somehow)

In a cupful of seawater, might've worked
Nicely in this respect into
A post-1855 triolet, at the least, or

Villenelle: of course Whitman caught
The eagles air-borne but hotly under
The influence of gravity in

24

A fairly sado-masochistic, as he tells
It, bond. But that's not English.
Those gar-eagles or gryfalcons or

Whatever they've got over there I suppose
Don't do it that way, and you wouldn't
Want the poets to get fancifully

Salacious just to make a pound. But what
I meant to say was that yesterday (quite
A bit happened yesterday) I saw several

Pairs of dragonflies in what looked like
A more crucial involvement than dalliance
Taking, to broach a euphemism, their joy

Of the air: they were bound and motile --
Congressed and unabashed! I hope they
Enjoyed "it" as much as me -- I think

I could go live with the animals too --
There are certain kinds of élan
The human mechanism simply can't rise to --

I don't know about frogs or turtles, however --
I wouldn't want to take on just any
Other identity sight unseen, as it were:

I'm human enough to want to have
The possibilities investigated (a case in which
You'd want to be sure to get a raw deal).

25

Any serious examination of a swamp
Is likely to bog down in puzzlement
Before long; yet we go on, some of us,

Saying things like What I tell
Is precisely what it is -- it is
In the manner of my telling -- it

Gathers to the manner of my speaking,
Unobtained, still to be gathered in
The manner of any other outflinging

Gatheringness: I diminish nothing --
Yet the nothing of all that is
Is undiminished in the outvaunt of my

Gathering: -- saying 'I am free
In the ardors and contradictions of
The never-to-be-obtained' -- asseverating

'I would reclaim the ghostly language
Of the ancient earth.' There are the bank
Swallows, I've seen them, banking and

Swallowing; there are those little worms,
Helgrammitical, that clean the teeth of
A trap-swonked mouse's mouth; I've seen

A fingerling shine like hellfire in a heron's beak --
It all gets hot from where I am, as I understand it:
Oh the juice of usual things, common, if you're lucky.

26

Oh, so little of what we do
Eventually works into anything, it's
Amazing how extravagantly we praise

The operation that has so many built-in
Come-downs -- yet I'm all for praising it,
This yammering for and against

The final sputter or flash-out -- I look
Around and don't see anything else
Remotely capable of

Assuming such errant nakedness: name
Something half as voluble of its lacks
And I'm likely to turn on

It: -- What do we have? a few expendable
Spurts in lustful actions so
Potentially calescent it's a shame some

People have to think of it all as a waste --
So why not cut loose into the open,
Drift easy in the light

Of what you can never get for sure,
Accommodate the dark, stand trusty
In the mile-swaths of the wind in swampgrass,

Assume whatever you can in the spirit of giving-over?
-- Oh: I feel I ought to tell you I know
Evolution is a function of diversity --

27

Some algae waving crowds of hands, others
Stumps; some rufus grouse, some gray:
The plumage maybe bespeaking where few

Go walking, as if protectively to itself,
Deeper variance -- food preferences, hardihood
Or the scattered feathers of its obverse, dullardry

Or bamboozling refinements of vision
In the keenest white of winter,
Salutatorian quickness or excellencies

Of flight so broken they give on grass
And willow thickets generation cries
No dead thing can gainsay the perking true of --

I know such needful groping
Aft of the right tailfeathers, fury
In the ambience of a special, maybe fatal,

49

Urine's perfume, generates multeity
Limited plottings can't contain, can't confound:
I feel how confections quickened into wriggling

May realize themselves somewhere down the river
In the hungry heart of the last moccasin
Watering there: how hunger produces loss

It either frets about or doesn't: how
Gutted to transformation, shat out, viable, risen
Beyond weeds or misty as the sunny rime of earth,

28

We get on: as if our choice were choice,
As if our presence at moonrise flattered the screech
Owl's screech, startled the marten to hunger,

Dismissed the tide from the headland -- as if
Our reach toward unity were more than song.
-- Oh there have been times, mornings

Broken from their newness, afternoons
In the maculation of a ridgeslope's sun and shade,
When I've studied the poise of a fox,

Its nose tuned for the kill; when
I've watched the goshawk, its whitefreckled
Underneath lightvibrant in the aspen

Green, rise; when I've looked for a long while
At the gargoyle merged in color and shape
With its snagperch, its eyes working

Like a spotting scope, gently setting its wings;
When the cottontail's cowered-forth
Nibbling away, from the known shadow

Of its deadfall, ears flexing persnickity
As a snail's antennae, feeling out
Into the greenshag bristling the open,

The unshieldedness of the glade, sounding
The precincts of the unseeable for
A clawrasp against rock, on talonloosened bark,

29

For the recomposing grass
Swish, after something has passed through . . .
I wander down along the railroad bank

Near Royal Gorge, where the elderberry wild
In its manyness plumes mid-Ozark summer
With the white splays of its flowering,

I can feel you here, down in the hot
Moist-hot dark
Dank under the elderberry's blooming --

Take me in only a little, just a little
Now into your shade, you willowy something
Plaiting like mist through the willows:

I need some time to go
Out to the marsh where the bittern is
And seldom seen, where the ducks come over

Low toward dark, their wings making a nigh
Silent thresh as they pass. Are we here
To render back what we have taken,

What we are hard at taking, before the venture
Of aeons takes each single separate venture
Into its way? Is unity the imperishable

Fire we cry for in our brokenness?
Is order the violence we call
Down on multeity, yowling

30

Out of the heights of our dread?   Turn
To the woodcock flushed tweetering from
Swampedge brush, the worms of its diet

Flighted as pinkbrown breast, bird heart,
Bat-like motility, winged! --
Where otherness gets and spends, torn and

Whole, where thaw-water's milky with frogseed
The old bonfire burns out of, burning on
Beyond the violence of our hallowing, beyond

The silence in the clattering of our dread --
Think of the buck grouse cocked for
The booming of his rutsong, his back

Feathering honeymackled in russet, his
Tailfan amber-lit in dawn spring light, spreaded
Vaunting as acknowledged lust, his neckruff

Cowled out, greenblack as a mallard drake's head:
Consider that crescendo of wing-music going
Out over the marshes the blue-winged teal

Gather to from the south again, where the starved
Doe fell in the blue wastage of February,
And thawing sloughed from her bones --

Be mindful of the fawns in their flimsy-limber
Heartihood, -- such booming ever-risen, rising
From the dwelling of the rhythms we're ventured to,

Beyond the prayers of our harrowing, from
Star to star, beyond the silence in
The music of our dread, from kindred

Sphere to sphere, I pray
From system on to system without end.
-- What is there, in the waste of what

We are, in the waste of our insistent
Systematic probes, that will never probe
In the waste of all our probing, to

The root of things? I can believe that
The sphere does not consist of a circuit
Which embraces, I can believe that

By feeling what I feel: I feel I will
Never be embraced by any circuit, I
Know I do not want to be embraced by

A circuit, I know that my knowing gladdens
From the things I know, as I know my
Knowing saddens from the things I know --

I am not a hero, fairly devoid of options,
In a scenario saying 'Take it, buddy,
Or starve on the lot.' How does one get

Out of the raggle-taggle of one's gettings?
How does one get the sphere of the unifying?
These are questions not to be asked in claptrap poetry.

When you come to the bluff
The new four-laner has made
Of a ridge in the mountains you feel

You know, don't get so
Happy that change has effected
Just this much altercation that

You don't go slow -- go slow --:
I'd like to see you tuckered-limp,
Plum sapless, inward-yelping toward

A promising rise again, so
I'll tell you what I saw -- the dog
Dropped skidding over the ledge of

The highway cut
And went with the roll of the talus out
Into the traffic --

The car in front of us caught
Him dead-center, where
He clunked on the ornate chrome,

Took the left front tire in the back
And flopped across the center stripe,
Head-bludgeoned spine-cracked and cut

Dead: my wife cried Oh
And not to be redundant I replied
I saw that coming.

33

I watch the hawks, sensing the possibility
Of a lesson in their outree wildness, feral
Implacability we like to feel

Is there, rising at least over the white
Wind ranges of the mind --
I particularly like the way they loft

Mild on the morning's warmth of wind, concealing
Need with motions that resemble leisure,
But raking the coulees, scrub pine, cornfields

Where the corn snake and field mice are
With rising hunger - and I like especially
The way they have of not going too

High, of anchoring ascent at a precise
Depth from the empty extensions of air:
For higher would prove the telescopic

Increment of sight loses its blessing,
The stoop to feeding would be too far,
A descent from nothing to

Nothing - the steady bleakness, broken
By danger, that isn't too bad when we're full -
While lower would show a view

Too total in its brokenness, concealing
The jackrabbit browsing too far from sage
In the dry wash draw

34

I'm concerned with risings, fast
Getaways that resolve themselves
In leisurely perk jerkings, accepted

Pecking orders, berry picking -
The almost bombastic get out
That justifies itself by working:

I like the way a cock pheasant
Caught napping in a woodlot's corner will
Decide against the 360 x N to the nth power

Number of lateral egresses from a well
Swung shotgun's version of infinity
And flush straight up, breaking his way to

Height, wrecking a shaft of the understory
Warblers might have taken yellow delight in
Frittering flycatching prissy ditties from --

Accelerating in gaudy kuk-yukking cry
Straight up, up out of the last
Frozen moment of utter discombobulation, till

Topping the trees
He brakes, backflips
and cuts flat-out for heavy cover --

As if the scratchfeed back of the barn,
Roadgrit, drainage ditch, and
Dickcisselling alfalfa never were.

35

I have come to take an interest in
The redwing black bird's quarrelling from
A spring swamp's tamarack stump --

How it adorns the wet air with a clarity
Iteration and the violent probabilities
That grow with the nights of the earth's

Turning might have something to do with --
I have come to take an interest in
Those versions of ongoingness that largely

Go on unseen: the cock woodcock's upward
Spiraling hosanna, that horny love song
Made of air and the windharps of his wings.

The stillness at the peak of want and song,
At the uttermost of his barrenness, that
Hovering at the nexus of his acres-wide based

Triangle woven in three dimensions at least
By the circles and ellipses of his rising lust;
Then the liquid twittering falling as from

Nowhere from that height, not straight
Down, but cutting through the prior arabesques
To land nearly where he started from --

Where dark lets the moon in to the aspen nubbins,
Where the horned owl gives the white pines half their dark,
Where the henbird waits like a clump of the wet, rich swamp.

36

Oh I know it's unwise to de-emphasize
That portion of the plenum
Where long-range answers get problems

Anxiously formulated on them, where
Women think its the berries to get
French stinkum at fifty bucks a bottle,

And sociologists tell us that
Suburbia is the frontier of the future:
Still, I work out my country --

I like to cut loose from my vacuum
Sealed humidor canister, Kentucky
Burley and Virginia Bright tobaccos,

And try for ways my maundersome loci
In woodlots or along the woodviolet fringing
Of entrepeneur-eyed swamps can show

A bit of how ontogeny recapitulates phylogeny --
I want to feel seawater sometimes almost
Capsize my corporate cytology: a covert's

Worth of the paleolithic wouldn't unsystematize
Things much: look, how the brown snake
Of the sandhill crane's neck sways at its feeding

In spring's winteramber corn! Look, how the sap bleeds
From the buckrubbed sapling last fall's bucklust bled!
I need something to sanctify the modern pipe smoker's needs.